A Spell of Trouble

ALAN MACDONALD

Illustrated by David Mostyn

OXFORD
UNIVERSITY PRESS

OXFORD
UNIVERSITY PRESS

Great Clarendon Street, Oxford OX2 6DP

Oxford University Press is a department of the University of Oxford.
It furthers the University's objective of excellence in research, scholarship,
and education by publishing worldwide in

Oxford   New York
Auckland   Cape Town   Dar es Salaam   Hong Kong   Karachi
Kuala Lumpur   Madrid   Melbourne   Mexico City   Nairobi
New Delhi   Shanghai   Taipei   Toronto

With offices in
Argentina   Austria   Brazil   Chile   Czech Republic   France   Greece
Guatemala   Hungary   Italy   Japan   Poland   Portugal   Singapore
South Korea   Switzerland   Thailand   Turkey   Ukraine   Vietnam

Oxford is a registered trade mark of Oxford University Press
in the UK and in certain other countries

Text © Alan MacDonald 1999

The moral rights of the author have been asserted

Database right Oxford University Press (maker)

First published 1999
This edition 2005

British Library Cataloguing in Publication Data
Data available

ISBN: 978-0-19-918431-6

9 10

Available in packs
Stage 15 Pack of 6:
ISBN: 978-0-19-918426-2
Stage 15 Class Pack:
ISBN: 978-0-19-918433-0
Guided Reading Cards also available:
ISBN: 978-0-19-918435-4

Cover artwork by David Mostyn

Printed in Great Britain by
Ashford Colour Press, Gosport Hants

Paper used in the production of this book is a natural, recyclable product
made from wood grown in sustainable forests. The manufacturing process
conforms to the environmental regulations of the country of origin.

1

The secret in the cellar

'I'm not going to school any more,'
announced Franklin.

He was sitting at his gran's kitchen table
with his chin propped in his hands. Franklin
often stopped by Granny Fay's house on his
way home from school. His gran always had
time to listen to his problems and, even
better, a full tin of chocolate biscuits in her
cupboard. Franklin took a fourth one and
spoke with his mouth full.

'Fey all pickomee. Iff not fair.'

'Who picks on you? That teacher again, Mr Lummocks?'

'Mr Lumsden,' corrected Franklin. 'Like today, I wasn't doing anything, nothing at all – just drawing. And he told me off in front of the whole class.'

'What were you drawing?'

'A headless ghost.'

'Splendid! Plenty of blood?'

'Buckets. The head was under his arm and dripping from the neck.'

Gran stroked her enormous cat, Jackson, under the chin. 'When I was at school, I got a merit award for my work on ghosts,' she said.

Not for the first time, Franklin wondered what kind of school his gran had gone to. He took another biscuit.

'And that wasn't the worst, Gran. At lunchtime we played football. And this boy in my class, Niall Foster … remember I told you about him?'

Gran nodded. 'Know-all Niall.'

'Yes, Know-all hates having me on his team, so he made me play in goal. Everyone knows I'm no good in goal.'

'You should tell him, Franklin.'

'I tried. I told him. But he's ten times as big as me, Gran. And he's always picking on me. He even said – you won't believe this – he said something about you.'

'What about me?'

'He says you're a witch!'

Gran choked on her tea, spilling some on Jackson's head.

'Obviously a complete dim-wit. What on earth made him say a thing like that?'

'He's seen you out shopping in your black cloak.'

'It's called a cape, Franklin.'

'Cape then. And there's Jackson. Witches always have black cats.'

'And I suppose he's seen me riding my broomstick across the moon? And mixing up spells in my cauldron?'

'I know it's dumb, Gran. I'm just telling you what Niall said.'

'Well, he'd better not come round here, or I might put a spell on him.'

For a moment Franklin stared. Gran burst out laughing.

'Don't look so worried, Franklin, it was a joke. Now before I forget, your mum asked to borrow one of my knitting patterns. You wait here while I look for it upstairs. I know I left it somewhere.'

Granny Fay put Jackson down and clumped up the stairs. Left alone, Franklin stood up. He was still hungry. Maybe he'd take a peek in Gran's cupboard. It was then he noticed that the cellar door wasn't closed properly.

The cellar was a forbidden place. As a rule, Gran kept the door locked. No one was allowed down, not even Franklin. Gran said the steps were dangerous and the light didn't work.

Franklin peered down into the darkness.

He had always been curious to see what Gran kept in her cellar. Whenever he asked her about it, she seemed to have a sudden attack of deafness.

'Another cup of tea, Franklin?' she would ask, as if he hadn't said anything.

Jackson nosed past him, brushing against his legs. Franklin gave him a gentle shove with his foot. 'Scram, fatso!' he said.

The cat disappeared, with a hiss, down the steps. That settled it. He could always say he was trying to rescue Jackson.

Taking the torch from the back of the door, Franklin started down the steps.

The cellar had a sweet, musty smell. Half-way down, he ducked into a cobweb. A spider, the size of his hand, scuttled across the ceiling. Franklin shuddered and went on, shining the torchlight to see his way.

Reaching the bottom, he was surprised to find the cellar opened out into a large room. Gran's old boiler creaked and groaned in one corner.

The room was warm and lit by candles. Franklin wondered why the candles hadn't burnt down. There were some bits of furniture; a faded armchair, and a grandfather clock, still ticking.

A *miaow* came from behind him. Franklin shone his torch and Jackson's green eyes glittered in the beam.

The cat was sitting on top of a shelf stacked with old books. Franklin had never seen anything like them. Each book was as big as a Bible and bound in red leather. He pulled one out with an effort. Wiping the dust from the cover, he could make out the title in strange, curly lettering:

A Booke of
Spelles and Curses
Volume 5

Franklin caught his breath. It was a book of magic. He turned the gold-edged pages. 'A spell for curing warts … A spell to make your ears grow … A curse for a plague of frogs …'

So it was true: his gran really was a witch. Franklin's head was reeling. All these years she had kept it from him. And now he'd stumbled on her secret in the cellar.

Just then Franklin heard his gran's footsteps overhead. She was coming down the stairs. What would she do if she found out he'd discovered her secret? Franklin turned cold with panic. She might even put a witch's spell on him.

2

Franklin tidies up

Franklin raced up the cellar steps, two at a time. He hung the torch back on the door and shut it behind him.

He could hear his gran in the hallway. Any second now, she would open the kitchen door and see him clutching her book of spells.

Franklin grabbed his school bag off the floor and jammed the book inside. It only just fitted. The bag bulged suspiciously at the sides. He was just about to fasten the straps, when Gran opened the door.

'I've found it!' she said.

'You have?' said Franklin, dropping the bag, guiltily. Witches had second sight. Perhaps she knew what he'd been up to. He looked around for a way of escape.

Gran was saying, 'I couldn't think where I'd left it but then I remembered. It was on the mirror on my dressing table. I put it up there with sticky tape so I wouldn't forget.'

'Um … forget what?' asked Franklin.

'The knitting pattern, what else? Look, this is the one your mum wanted. Isn't that a lovely cardigan?'

'Oh yes, great,' said Franklin, breathing a sigh of relief.

'I'll put it in your school bag, shall I, so you don't lose it?'

'Yes … NO! No, don't put it in there!' He grabbed the bag out of Gran's hands.

She shrugged. 'Okay, no need to shout, Franklin. Is there something you don't want me to see in there?'

'No, nothing! I mean … well … just something I've been making at school.'

'I see,' said Gran, 'it's a surprise is it? I understand. I was always giving my parents surprises at your age.'

I bet you were, thought Franklin.

'Have some more tea before you go,' offered Gran.

'No, no thanks,' said Franklin. He was edging towards the door. 'I'd better get this knitting pattern back to Mum – in case it's urgent.'

'It's for Christmas, Franklin. That's months away.'

'Still, I'd better be off, Gran. Thanks for the um ... chat.'

* * *

At home, Franklin ran straight upstairs to his bedroom. He couldn't wait to try out something from the book.

'Franklin, is that you?' his mum called after him.

'Yes, Mum.'

'You're late home.'

'I stopped to see Gran.'

'Well, your dinner's nearly ready. You'd better start tidying your room. Don't forget it's got to be done tonight.'

'I'm doing it now,' lied Franklin. His mum was always going on at him about the state of his bedroom.

He shut the door and wedged a chair against it.

Taking the book of spells from his bag, he laid it carefully on his bed: a real magic book. He still couldn't quite believe he had it.

All these years his gran had pretended to be a dotty old lady when, really, she was a witch. Now he thought about it, lots of things made sense. Like the way his gran always seemed to be expecting him when he arrived. Like the way she acted so funny about anyone going in her cellar. Like her stories about her school days: her pet toad, Spot, who slept in her bed, and Miss Ivy, the teacher who kept disappearing in the middle of lessons.

And now he had Gran's book of spells – all the power he ever wanted in his hands – if only he could make the spells work.

That bit worried him. What if he couldn't understand the instructions? Or what if the spells only worked for real witches?

Fingers trembling, Franklin opened the book at page one.

'No 1 – A Spelle for Household Chores

Witches have far better things to do than wash up dirty cauldrons all day. Here's a spell to use for general cleaning and tidying – especially handy if you've got a few old crones coming round for supper, the pot's bubbling and your hovel is a mess.

The spell is a simple one. Spit three times on your palms, rub them together and repeat the words ...'

Franklin was interrupted by a knock on the door.

'Franklin? What are you doing in there?'

His mum – couldn't she leave him alone for even five minutes?

'Nothing, Mum.'

'That's just what I thought. You're supposed to be tidying your room.'

'I am. I've done loads.'

'I bet. Let's see ...' His mum tried the door handle. 'Let me in. What have you got against this door, Franklin?'

'Sorry, the handle must be stuck.'

18

'Open this door! And if you haven't made a start, Franklin, there'll be big trouble.'

Why did mums always say that, 'BIG trouble'? Franklin was always in BIG trouble. He would have welcomed some small trouble for a change.

He glanced at his room. The carpet was buried under piles of comics, socks, CDs, computer games and last week's underpants. Franklin's uniform had only made it halfway to the wardrobe. His school-bag was where he'd thrown it, scattering papers and books across his bed.

The spell claimed to work for any kind of cleaning or tidying. Could he make it work now? If he didn't, he was in trouble – big trouble – as usual.

Quickly, he spat three times on his palms and rubbed them together.

'Franklin! I'm getting cross. Open this door!' called his mum.

Franklin recited the spell from the book.

'Spick and span, morning dew
Make this room as clean as new.'

Next moment, he had to duck as books, socks, comics and trainers started to fly up off the floor. They came together in a whirlwind, sucking everything upwards towards the ceiling: pillows, duvet and computer, jumpers, underpants, light bulbs …

Everything was whirling around in the air. Sparks of blue and silver bounced off the walls.

Franklin dived under the bed. What had he done? It was terrifying!

'Franklin! What's going on in there?' yelled his mum, rattling the door. 'Let me in!'

A second later, the whirlwind stopped. Everything fell down from the ceiling and landed neatly in its place. Drawers opened to catch clothes. His duvet and pillows floated back on to the bed. The computer set itself down on his desk, with all his games neatly stacked in a pile.

When Franklin crawled out from under the bed, his room was so tidy he didn't recognize it.

'Wow!' said Franklin in a daze. 'It works! I can do magic.'

The door handle rattled again. He hid the book under his pillow and let in his mum.

'I don't know what you've been up to, Franklin, but …'

Her voice trailed away. She gazed around the room in boggle-eyed wonder.

'Well?' said Franklin, 'I told you I'd tidied up.'

'But how did you …? Where are all the …? And it's so … clean!'

His mum sat down, heavily, in a chair. Franklin lay back on his bed and stretched out, enjoying his triumph.

'From now on, Mum,' he said with a mysterious smile, 'I'm going to be a different person.'

He didn't know how right he was.

3

Snakes alive!

Early next morning, Granny Fay rang the door-bell at Franklin's house.

Franklin's mum answered the door.

'Oh, hello, Mum,' she said to Granny Fay. 'You're up early. I'm afraid I can't stop, I'm just off to work.'

'It's your Franklin I want to see,' said Granny Fay, grimly. 'It's important. He's got something of mine.'

'Oh. You've just missed him, I'm afraid. He went to school five minutes ago.'

Gran looked at her watch. 'But it's only eight-fifteen. School doesn't start till nine.'

'I know. He hardly ate any breakfast. Said he wanted to get to school early this morning. It's not like him at all.'

'Ahh,' said Granny Fay, and, 'Oh, I see.'

'What's he done this time? You seem a bit upset.'

'Oh, no, it's nothing really. He just borrowed one of my books, that's all.'

'Without asking, I bet.'

'Well, yes ...'

'I don't know what goes on in that boy's head. I'll get him to pop it round straight after school and apologize.'

'It's just an old book full of nonsense, nothing to worry about,' said Granny Fay, brightly. She guessed Franklin had the book with him.

Her smile faded as she turned away. What did he want with a book of spells at school?

* * *

Franklin had left the house early that morning for a reason. He knew that Niall Foster's gang met in the playground to play football before school.

The book of spells was in his school bag. He knew one or two useful spells off by heart already, and Know-all Niall was just the person to try them on.

He found him in the playground with his pals.

'Hiya Niall!' said Franklin, cheerfully.

'Bug out, Franklinstein. We're just about to kick off.'

'Great. I'll play.'

'You won't. Duffers aren't allowed in this game.'

'How come you're playing then, Niall?'

Niall gave Franklin his cold stare. 'Is that supposed to be a joke, Franklinstein? Are you trying to be funny?'

'Look,' said Franklin, 'who's the captain here? No, let me guess – you are, Niall.'

'Right. And I wouldn't pick you if you got down on your knees and begged me. So out of the way, maggot-brains.'

Niall put the ball down to kick off. Franklin didn't stand aside as Niall expected. Instead, he actually put his foot on the ball.

'I've got an idea,' Franklin said, 'why don't I be captain today?'

'Get your foot off the ball,' warned Niall.

'Think about it, Niall, you're always the captain ...'

'Get your foot off the ball …'

'… so why don't we swap? I'll be captain and I won't pick you, just so you know what it feels like. Because if you want to know, Niall, my granny's cat could beat you at football.'

There was a dead silence. Niall's gang looked at their leader. They all knew Niall wasn't as great at football as he thought – but no one had ever dared say so. Niall picked up the ball and advanced on Franklin.

'I wouldn't throw that,' warned Franklin.

'Yeah? Or what? You gonna get me, Franklinstein?'

Franklin hoped the spell worked. If it didn't, Niall was going to flatten him. Backing away, he chanted:

Maggots, flies and fish in the rivers
Change this ball to something that slithers.'

Suddenly, the football went cold in Niall's hands. It started to grow and stretch itself out. The black spots on the ball became dark scales. Before his eyes, the ball began to coil.

Niall dropped it in horror. 'Yeaaah!
A snake! It's a snake!'

Franklin watched him back off. Then
Know-all Niall turned and ran.

'I warned you, Niall,' shouted Franklin,
after him, 'don't mess with me. I'm magic!'

* * *

Mr Lumsden was not pleased. The class sat in silence while he went on with his lecture.

'And whoever *does* know had better tell me. Bringing pets into school is against the rules. But a snake – I don't happen to find that funny. A number of children were very scared. Melanie Wimborn has had to go and lie down. She had a nasty shock when the snake got into the girls' toilets.'

Franklin smiled to himself. Melanie Wimborn was the class tell-tale. For once she had a tale worth telling.

'Franklin Hobbs!' Mr Lumsden's voice boomed out.

'Yes, sir?'

'You find that amusing, do you?'

'No, sir.'

'Wipe that silly smirk off your face then.'

'Yes, sir.'

Know-all Niall stood up and pointed at Franklin. 'It was Franklin did it, sir. I saw him. I was showing him my football, when he started jabbering. Then the ball changed into a snake. Or the snake came out of the ball, I dunno. But Franklin did it. We all saw him.'

Other people were nodding: Ben Shaw and Ryan Grace who were in Niall's gang.

'That's right, sir. It was Franklin. He did it.'

Mr Lumsden turned his gaze on Franklin. 'Well, Franklin, what have you got to say? Do you know something about this snake?'

'N... no, sir.'

'Everyone else seems to think you do.'

Franklin felt the eyes of the whole class upon him. He hesitated.

Lumsden bellowed at him, 'I'm waiting, boy! Stand up and speak up! Was it you that brought this snake into school? YES OR NO?'

Franklin stood up. Lumsden was picking on him again. His mouth had gone dry. Everyone was waiting for him to answer.

'No, sir, I didn't bring any snake into school,' he said, quietly.

'Very well, Franklin. I want you and Niall to see me at break-time. We're going to get to the bottom of this, if it takes all day.'

'Yes, sir.' Franklin sat down with relief. He'd told the truth after all. He hadn't brought the snake into school. He'd only brought a book of spells.

People were still looking at him. Know-all Niall caught his eye and drew a finger across his throat. That meant his gang would be waiting for Franklin at break. And before that, he had to see Lumsden.

It was all the teacher's fault. Why did he have to pick on him? Why couldn't he pick on someone else for a change? Franklin hated standing up in front of the whole class. He couldn't think straight with everyone staring at him.

He scowled at Mr Lumsden who was now handing out maths books.

'How would you like it if you got picked on?' he said, quietly.

Taking care no one was watching, Franklin slid the book of spells out of his bag.

4

Which one's Franklin?

Franklin turned the pages of the book of spells on his lap. It was time he taught Mr Lumsden a lesson. Nobody picked on Franklin Hobbs and got away with it.

He found the spell he was looking for and said it in a whisper.

'Moon in winter, stars in space,
Make the body change its place.'

Next moment, Franklin felt he was being turned inside out. It was a very odd feeling – as if his body was leaving him.

When it stopped, he looked around. The classroom was still there, but somehow he had moved places. Instead of sitting at his desk, he was standing at the front of the class.

And where had Lumsden vanished to? The spell was meant for him. Franklin's gaze swept over the class. His eyes came to rest on his own place.

Sitting in his seat was a boy who was his exact double! The boy was staring at his hands in a bewildered way. So if that boy was Franklin, who was he? He had a horrible feeling he knew. He left the room and ran to the boys' toilets.

There was a mirror over the sink. Franklin gasped at his reflection. The face he saw looking back at him was not his, but Mr Lumsden's.

Franklin touched it with his fingers. There was the creepy, caterpillar moustache. There were the beetle-black eyebrows. His wrists had hair growing on them too. And he was so tall, he had to bend down to see himself in the mirror.

There was no doubting it. The spell had gone disastrously wrong. He had meant Mr Lumsden to turn into a boy. But instead, Franklin had changed bodies with his teacher! He was inside Mr Lumsden's body! Which meant that the boy who looked like him must be Mr Lumsden.

'Oh no, no, no! What have I done?' moaned Franklin.

This time he really was in BIG trouble.

When he got back to the classroom, some of the class were out of their seats.

'Sit down immediately!' thundered Franklin. He hadn't mean to shout. His own booming voice took him by surprise. Even more surprising was the effect on the class. They flocked back to their seats like frightened sheep.

Franklin felt a new sense of power. No one had ever obeyed him before!

One boy was still wandering around at the front of the class. It was the one who looked like him – Mr Lumsden in Franklin's body.

From force of habit, Mr Lumsden sat down in the teacher's seat. He hadn't yet realized he'd changed into a schoolboy. Franklin decided he'd better get rid of him quickly.

'Franklin!' he said, standing over him. 'You are sitting in *my* seat.'

The class started to giggle. Mr Lumsden got up, utterly confused.

'I've got to take the lesson,' he murmured.

'Oh, really?' said Franklin. 'Listen, everybody. Franklin is going to take the lesson.'

It was wonderful. Making fun of people was easy.

'Turn to page 15 in your maths books,' said Mr Lumsden in a squeaky voice.

The class rocked with laughter. This was a great joke: Franklin Hobbs standing at the front, pretending to be a teacher.

Mr Lumsden blinked at them, completely lost. Why didn't they listen to him? Why did his voice sound high and anxious?

Franklin put a hand on Mr Lumsden's shoulder. 'That'll do, Franklin – back to your seat. And don't let me catch you out of it again.'

Mr Lumsden walked back to his place in a daze.

At that moment, the bell went for morning break. Franklin waited for the class to go, but they stayed in their seats looking at him expectantly. Finally, it dawned on him. They were waiting for his permission to leave. 'All right, class,' he said, 'you may go.'

They got up and left the room. It was amazing. Franklin said 'sit down' and they sat down. He said 'stand up' and they stood up. Even Niall Foster's gang – the terrors of the playground – obeyed him.

Perhaps changing himself into a teacher wasn't such a bad move after all. He could always change himself back whenever he wanted. And meanwhile, he could do what he liked.

Franklin had often wondered what it was like to be a teacher: now he knew. It was like being a giant surrounded by midgets. He was in charge. The class would do anything he told them.

Franklin looked around for the book of spells and found it under his old desk.

Locking it carefully in his teacher's drawer, he noticed Niall Foster, watching him from the doorway.

'Niall!' Franklin took a step back. For a moment he thought Niall had come to get him. But he was forgetting he was now a teacher.

Niall said, 'You wanted to see me and Franklin, sir, at break, you said.'

'Did I? Oh yes, I did.' Franklin remembered now. Mr Lumsden had asked to see both of them about the snake business. That was before the spell had made them swap places.

Niall smiled unpleasantly. 'Franklin ran off, sir, to the playground, sir. Do you want me to get him?'

'No, come in and shut the door, Niall,' said Franklin.

Here was the perfect chance for his revenge on Know-all Niall; Niall who called him Franklinstein, who made fun of him, who had once sat on his chest and made him eat grass.

Here was Know-all without his gang,
looking small and nervous. Franklin bent
down to look him in the eye.

'I know all about you, Niall Foster,' he said.

Niall blinked. 'Pardon, sir?'

'I know what you get up to when you
think I can't see you.'

'Sir? I don't do nothing, sir.'

'Don't you? Pushing to the front of the queue at dinner times. Picking on smaller children – making them eat grass. Why does your gang call themselves The Torturers, Niall?'

Niall's ears had turned red. There was nothing he could say. It was all true. But how could Mr Lumsden know all this?

'From now on, I'm going to be keeping my eye on you, Niall,' said Franklin. 'And if I ever catch you picking on anyone, there'll be trouble – BIG trouble. Do I make myself clear?'

Niall nodded, his face white as chalk.

'And as for this story about me … I mean Franklin,' he corrected himself quickly, 'as for this story about Franklin turning a ball into a snake, I've never heard such whopping great lies.'

'But sir …'

'Quiet, Niall! I won't have you telling tales to get other children into trouble. Now go out into the playground. I want you to pick up every piece of litter you can find.'

Niall's jaw dropped.

'I'll be out to inspect your work later,' warned Franklin.

Niall was about to protest, but one look at his teacher's face changed his mind. He left the room, closing the door, quietly, behind him.

Franklin sat down with his feet on top of the desk. He burst out laughing. Being a teacher was going to be fun.

5

A teacher's nightmare

Out in the playground, the real Mr Lumsden was not enjoying himself. He kept close to the railings. The playground was noisy and he felt painfully small.

He only ever came out here on playground duty. Then he would patrol the groups of children, keeping an eye out for mischief.

But it all looked different from down here; a jungle of legs, elbows and noises. Some girls ran past, screaming at the tops of their voices. A football cannoned off a wall, narrowly missing his head.

Lumsden flattened himself against the railings. Maybe if he closed his eyes, he would wake up. He would be back at the front of the class, teaching. It was all just a bad dream.

'Franklin!' a voice hissed near his ear.

He opened his eyes. An old woman was staring at him through the railings. Her grey wispy hair was tied back in a bun. She had piercing blue eyes and a black cape wrapped around her. Mr Lumsden thought she looked slightly mad.

'Where is it?' she demanded. 'I want it back.'

'Where's what? I don't know what you're talking about!' said Mr Lumsden, truthfully.

'You know perfectly well, you stole it from my cellar.'

'What cellar? I've never even met you!'

'Don't play games, Franklin. Your gran is a witch, don't forget. I may be retired, but I still know how to use magic.'

The old bat was obviously bonkers.

Though he had to admit she did look like a witch. Mr Lumsden thought he'd better go and fetch a teacher.

'Don't you walk away from me, my lad!' said the old woman, sternly.

He stopped in his tracks.

'Please! I don't know who you are. I don't even know who *I* am. Please, just leave me alone.'

'Not till I get back my book of spells. Volume five: what have you done with it?'

'I haven't got any book!'

'Where have you hidden it?'

'I told you, I haven't got it!'

'I'm warning you, Franklin, either you give it back, or I'll be forced to use magic. I don't wish to, but I will. The choice is yours.'

Lumsden shook his head. It wasn't fair. Why was everyone picking on him? First the teacher and the class laughing at him; now this mad old lady, raving about magic.

He turned his back on her and walked away.

Next minute, he felt his feet lifted off the ground. The playground and its noises melted away. Instead, he seemed to be hurtling over rooftops in a blur of speed.

It all happened in seconds. When he'd
stopped trembling, Lumsden realized he was
sitting in somebody's house. A fire crackled in
the grate. A huge, sour-faced black cat was
curled on the hearth rug. In the armchair,
opposite, sat the mad old woman with her
arms folded.

'Now Franklin,' she said, 'I'll ask you one
last time. Where is my book of spells?'

6

Flying lessons

At that moment, Mr Lumsden might have
been surprised to see what was happening
back at school. The book of spells was open
on the teacher's desk. Franklin was teaching
his first lesson from it.

'Who can tell me what gravity is?' asked
Franklin, smiling.

No one put up their hand. Niall Foster
avoided his gaze. His back ached from
picking up litter.

'Gravity is one of those laws you learn in science,' said Franklin, walking round the class. 'It says that what goes up, must come down. Shall we try a little experiment to see if that's true?'

The class shifted in their seats. Their teacher was acting very strangely today. He had a wild look in his eye.

Franklin chanted the words of a spell.

'Eagle's feather, raven's eye
Bring to us the gift to fly.'

Immediately it happened.

The class rose out of their seats and floated towards the ceiling. Niall Foster tried to hang on to his chair but it just came with him.

'You see! Gravity is wrong!' whooped Franklin in triumph. 'What is down, must go up!'

He turned a somersault in the air.

Several of the class clung to each other in case they fell. Melanie Wimborn started to whimper.

'Don't be such a baby, Melanie,' said
Franklin. 'Enjoy yourself. Try a loop the loop!'

There was a knock on the door. A
bespectacled face looked in. Mrs Gammage,
the head, had come to ask Mr Lumsden if
he'd cleared up the snake business. At first
she was puzzled by the rows of empty desks
in the room. Then looking up, she discovered
Class 3 gaping down at her from the ceiling.

'Mr Lumsden! What in heaven's name is going on?'

'Just a little science experiment,' replied Franklin from the ceiling. 'We're testing the law of gravity.'

'Get those children down at once!'

'Er … well, I'm not sure if I can,' said Franklin. He hadn't read that far in the book.

Mrs Gammage caught hold of Franklin's trouser leg and tried to pull him down.

'Ow! Leggo! Get off me!' shouted Franklin.

Mrs Gammage tugged harder. Franklin wasn't ready to come down yet but his trousers were. He could feel them slipping down. He wondered what kind of underwear Mr Lumsden wore. To spare his blushes, he did the only thing he could think of. He aimed a spell at the headteacher.

'Lightning bolt and thunderstorm
Take away this mortal form.'

A second later, Mrs Gammage vanished. In her place, stood a large rhinoceros wearing glasses and a flowery dress.

'Crumbs!' said Franklin. 'Sorry, Mrs Gammage, I must have got my spells mixed up!'

The rhinoceros started to blunder angrily around the room, knocking over desks and chairs. On the ceiling, the class buzzed around like frightened bluebottles. Melanie Wimborn hung on to the light-fitting and wailed, 'I want to go hooome!'

Franklin felt that his first lesson wasn't going quite to plan. He flew over to open one of the top windows.

'Keep calm, class,' he shouted. 'Everyone follow me outside!'

* * *

Outside, Franklin tried to gather his class over the school car park. He counted them. They were all there, except Mr Lumsden. It was typical of the teacher to go off with Franklin's body, just when he needed it back. But right now, Franklin had other worries. Some of his class were flying off to chase pigeons.

'Er … try and keep together!' called Franklin. 'I'll have you down in just a minute.'

Below, the car park was beginning to fill up with people. Teachers were hurrying their classes out of the main doors. Franklin had a nasty feeling the rhino had something to do with it.

Tracey Burns, of Class 2, spotted something in the sky. 'Look!' she pointed, 'that's Mr Lumsden's class! What are they doing up there?' Other faces turned skywards to look.

Franklin, up above, heard voices calling him to come down. He wanted to obey, but he couldn't. He didn't know the right spell and he'd left his gran's book behind. He tried to think. Maybe he should recite the spell backwards. That might undo it.

He closed his eyes and tried to remember:
'Er … fly to gift … um … us to call …
Eye raven, feather eagle.'
Nothing happened. Except that when he

opened his eyes, Franklin nearly collided
with the school bell tower. He grabbed hold
of it and held on for dear life. Glancing
down, he saw the ground, a dizzy distance
below. People were scurrying around like
ants. Voices told him to hang on. Franklin
wasn't thinking of doing anything else.

He was relieved to hear footsteps coming up the staircase. Mr Thomas, the deputy head, appeared.

Strong arms grabbed him by the waist and pulled him inside. Once he had his feet on solid ground, the floating stopped. Maybe the law of gravity was right after all: what goes up, must sooner or later come down.

* * *

At the bottom of the tower, he found the whole school waiting for him. Worried teachers crowded round him, all talking at once.

'Mr Lumsden, what the devil is going on?'

'Where is Mrs Gammage?'

'Who let that rhino loose?'

'How did your class get up there?'

'Can't you get them down?'

Franklin shielded his eyes and gazed into the sky. A few of his class were perched in the tree-tops, hanging on to the branches.

Niall Foster had his arms and legs wrapped

around the top of a lamp-post. The rest were drifting off, like coloured balloons, towards the town.

'That's my Melanie up there. She can't stand heights; they make her sick,' warned Mrs Wimborn, who had arrived from somewhere.

'Don't worry, I can sort it all out,' Franklin lied.

'Oh, *that's* all right then,' said Mrs Wimborn, with heavy sarcasm. 'Listen to this, everyone! Mr Lumsden is going to sort it all out!'

An expectant silence fell.

'No need to panic ...' said Franklin. 'I can bring the children down. It's just that I need a book – a sort of magic book in fact – which I've left somewhere ...'

Where? Where had he left it?

Mr Thomas had heard enough. 'I'm going to call the police,' he said, turning on his heel.

'And the fire brigade,' shouted Mrs Wimborn, after him. 'Tell them to bring a ladder.'

She jabbed a plump finger into Franklin's chest. 'This is all your fault! I'm going to make a complaint. I don't send my little girl to school to see her fly past my kitchen window. She's got Brownies tonight ...'

Franklin tried to think. The situation was like a nightmare. What if he couldn't undo the flying spell? That would mean he couldn't reverse any of the spells. And that meant he'd be stuck as a teacher for the rest of his life.

The idea horrified him: every day waking

up and seeing Mr Lumsden's face in the mirror, stuck with an itchy moustache and piles of dreary homework to mark.

Mrs Wimborn was still talking. 'What are you going to do about it?' she demanded. 'Come on, we're all waiting.'

Franklin opened his mouth to speak but he was interrupted by the sound of glass shattering. Evidently, the rhino was growing tired of being shut in a classroom.

With a sinking feeling, Franklin suddenly remembered exactly where he'd left the book of spells: on the teacher's desk in the classroom. If he wanted to undo the spells, he was going to have to go in and fetch it.

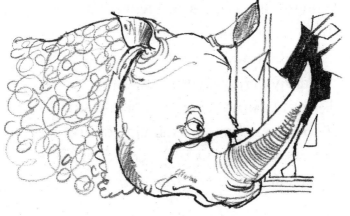

7

Rhino at large

Turning the handle slowly, Franklin let
himself in through the main school doors.
Everything was quiet inside. Perhaps the
rhino had exhausted itself and fallen asleep.
Or maybe it was in hiding, waiting for him.

Hardly daring to breathe, Franklin crept
down the corridor towards his classroom.
He could see the door hanging off its hinges
at a crazy angle. His shoes crunched on
broken glass.

The scene inside the classroom was worse than he'd imagined. The room looked as if it had been struck by a sudden earthquake. Chairs and tables lay overturned. Three of the lower windows were shattered. Pencils, rulers, powder paints and books were trampled on the floor.

But luckily, there was no sign of the rhino.

Mrs Gammage (Franklin had to remind himself it was really her) had obviously battered the door down to get out. He kept still and listened. Somewhere at the far end of the school, a chair scraped the floor.

It took a few minutes to find the book. It was underneath a mess of paint pots. Its red cover was stained yellow with powder paint, but otherwise it looked unharmed.

Franklin knew he should take it and leave as quickly as possible, but he was desperate to look inside. It would only take a few seconds and the rest of his life depended on the book. There had to be a way to undo the spells.

He flicked through rapidly, until he came to the spell he'd used on Mr Lumsden. Franklin read it right through, from beginning to end. There was no mention of how to reverse the spell. He turned the page: more spells, nothing about undoing them.

He was stuck in a never-ending nightmare: trapped in his teacher's body for the rest of his life!

Franklin raised his head slowly. Someone else was in the room with him. Out of the corner of one eye, he could see the huge, ugly rhino blocking the doorway. Its glasses were crooked and it was breathing heavily.

He tried to remember what you were supposed to do to prevent a rhino from charging. Was it stand stock still or stare it down?

He tried talking to it in a soothing way.
'Mrs Gammage – hi! It's me, Franklin Hobbs.
Listen, I'm not really Mr Lumsden and you're
not really a rhino – although I admit you do
look like one …'

The rhino lifted its massive head. Franklin
couldn't take his eyes off the mean-looking
horn.

'Look – would you like a biscuit? They've
got some in the staff room,' he said,
desperately. 'What sort do you like? Bourbons?
Custard creams? Or maybe, as a rhino, you'd
prefer a pot plant to chew, or something?
I think Mrs Gammage has got one.'

Maybe it wasn't the best thing to say.
At the mention of the pot plant, the rhino
lowered its horn. It was going to charge.
Franklin was sure of it.

He took a step back and stumbled over a
chair. The next moment, the rhino was
coming at him. He saw the angry, bloodshot
eyes – eyes like Mrs Gammage's – as he threw
himself to one side.

The rhino missed him and slammed into the wall behind. The remaining glass fell out of the window and the Venetian blinds came down, with a clatter, on its head. Snorting, the rhino shook itself free.

It turned back for Franklin, but Franklin was no longer there. He was leaping over the chairs and tables, trying to get out of the classroom. Once in the corridor, he sprinted to the main doors, with the book of spells clutched under one arm. From the way the floor was shaking, he could tell the rhino wasn't far behind.

8

Facing the magic

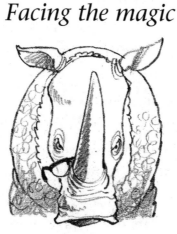

Bursting out of the doors, Franklin found his path blocked by teachers and children.

'Out of the way! It's after me!' he yelled.

He needn't have bothered. When they saw the rhino, the crowd scattered in every direction.

Franklin didn't stop running: he kept going for the main gates. Once he was through, he slammed them shut with a clang, and pushed the bolt across. He was just in time to see the rhino come pounding, angrily, across the car park.

'Stay there, Mrs Gammage,' he called back, 'I'm going to get help!'

Franklin knew only one person could help him. He set off running again, in the direction of the house.

Up above, he could see his class getting smaller in the distance. Soon they'd be out of sight. Maybe he'd never see any of them, ever again. Maybe Mrs Gammage would end up in a zoo; staring mournfully at school children through the bars of her cage. And it was all *his* fault.

He wished he'd never set eyes on the book of spells.

Two police cars flashed past him with sirens wailing. They were followed by a fire-engine, heading for the school.

'Oh please, *please* let her be in,' prayed Franklin, under his breath.

* * *

He reached the house and banged the cat's-head door knocker.

There was a pause which seemed to last for ages. Maybe Granny Fay was out. Franklin opened the letter-box. He was about to shout through it, when the door swung open.

He fell forward on his hands and knees and found himself nose to nose with Jackson. The big black cat eyed him scornfully.

'Gran! Gran, you've got to help me!' said Franklin, scrambling to his feet.

To his surprise, Franklin saw his gran had
another visitor. Someone was standing
behind her, someone who looked like
Franklin. It dawned on him that it was Mr
Lumsden. But what was he doing in Granny
Fay's house?

'You see,' Mr Lumsden was saying,
excitedly, 'he made us swap. *That's* your
grandson! Tell him to give my body back.'

Granny Fay picked up the book of spells from the floor. She gave Franklin a frosty glare. 'Well, Franklin, is that really you?'

'Yes, sorry, Gran, I'm really, really sorry,' was all Franklin could say.

Gran shook her head and picked up Jackson. 'You'd better come into the sitting-room.'

* * *

When Franklin had finished telling his story, Granny Fay pursed her lips.

'There's one thing you missed out,' she said. 'Why? I want to know why you stole the book in the first place.'

Franklin tried to remember. It had seemed like a good idea at the time.

'Everyone was picking on me,' he said, 'and I wanted to show them. I thought maybe if I had magic powers, people would look up to me.'

Gran sighed deeply. 'And what do you think now, Franklin?'

'I just want to be myself again,' pleaded Franklin. 'It's terrible being a teacher.'

'It's not much fun being a schoolboy,' said Mr Lumsden, bitterly. 'Everyone picks on you.'

'I know,' said Franklin. He turned to his Gran. 'I've made such a mess of it, Gran. Mrs Gammage is a rhino; my class are all floating away; and everyone thinks I'm Mr Lumsden! You've got to help me, please! I just want everything back the way it was before.'

Mr Lumsden nodded. 'Please, *please*, Mrs Fay.'

Gran looked at them both. 'Spells are funny things. It's easy to cast a few spells. Any fool can do that, even you, Franklin. It's not so easy to put things right afterwards.'

'You mean I'm stuck like this for the rest of my life?' wailed Franklin.

'I didn't say that. There is perhaps one way,' she said, tapping the magic book.

Franklin wondered what she was going to ask them to do. Eat a horny-backed toad? Sleep the night in a graveyard? But Granny Fay walked over to the fire and fingered the old leather book sadly.

'This is something I should have done a long, long time ago,' she said.

As soon as she tossed it into the fire, the book burst into crackling blue flames.

Franklin watched it curl and turn black at the edges. He began to feel something happening. His body was turning inside out again …

9

Franklin himself

A week later, Franklin called in again to see his gran.

'Come in, Franklin. Would you like a cup of tea? School as vile as ever? Chocolate biscuit?' asked Gran.

Franklin helped himself to three chocolate biscuits and ignored the tea. He spoke with his mouth full. 'Ith a fummy thigran ...'

'Again, without the biscuit,' said Gran, patiently. Franklin swallowed his mouthful.

'It's a funny thing, Gran, but no one at school seems to remember what happened. At least if they do, they never talk about it.'

'Of course they don't,' said Granny Fay. 'Who's going to believe them? Snakes and wild rhinos loose in the school? Children flying through the clouds? They think they imagined it all.'

'But they're acting dead funny. Like Mr Lumsden – he's gone all, well … nice. He doesn't shout or pick on you any more. And he's always out in the playground, making sure all the little kids are okay.'

Granny Fay smiled to herself, remembering the frightened boy she'd met by the railings.

'And you know Niall Foster?' continued Franklin.

'Know-all Niall?'

'Yes. He asked me if I wanted to play football today. I've noticed he looks over his shoulder all the time – as if he thinks someone's watching him to make sure he behaves.'

'Whoever could have put that idea in his head?'

'Don't ask me,' Franklin grinned.

'And what about your headteacher? Mrs Cribbage? Has she recovered?'

'Mrs Gammage? Oh yes, she's just the same, except that she's always stopping to look at herself in mirrors or windows. She keeps feeling her nose like this.'

Franklin did his impression of Mrs Gammage. He felt his nose, anxiously, to see if it was growing into a rhino horn.

Granny Fay laughed and clapped her hands. 'So things didn't turn out so bad, after all. But I trust you've learned your lesson, Franklin: no more playing with magic.'

Franklin nodded solemnly. 'Don't worry, Gran. I much prefer being myself to being Mr Lumsden.'

'I'm glad to hear it, because I prefer you that way too.'

Franklin went to take another bite of chocolate biscuit, then he paused, thoughtfully.

'One thing I've been wondering, Gran. That book of spells you burnt on the fire – it was volume five, wasn't it?'

'That's right.'

'And I saw at least six other volumes in your cellar. What have you done with them all?'

'Burnt them, of course,' said Gran, airily. 'It's what I should have done years ago, when I retired from witching.'

Franklin glanced in the direction of the cellar. He'd tried the door handle earlier. 'Then why do you still keep the cellar door locked, Gran, if there's nothing down there?'

Gran avoided his gaze. She bent down to stroke Jackson. 'Who's Grandma's baby then? Do you want another cup of tea, Franklin?'

It seemed that her temporary deafness had come on again.

About the author

When I was at school there was a boy rather like Franklin. He was always being picked on by his class teacher. In his case there was a reason – his teacher was also his mum!

Many of my stories come out of 'what if?' ideas. This story came from the thought, *What if a boy could swap places with his teacher?* Franklin thinks that being in a position of power will solve all his problems. But he soon discovers that teachers have problems of their own.